10 Easy-

MW01254196

Marcella Shaffer

CONTENTS

Introduction

Perennials are the wonder of the garden world and the heart of most flower gardens. They are well loved for the kaleidoscope of colors they offer, revered for their ability to flower and spread year after year, and treasured for the beauty of their form, texture, and foliage. They invite birds, butterflies, honeybees, and humans alike to come closer and admire their elegance and charm. They are the delight and passion of gardeners around the world.

There are thousands of garden perennials, and even more varieties are developed every year. Some are flashy and showy, dressed in screaming colors and exotic shapes. Others are simple yet elegant, expressions of a subtle beauty found in delicate foliage and geometric form. Some bear the dubious beauty of careful breeding, with giant showy heads that must be staked and propped. Others remain true to their hardy wildflower roots, with small perky blossoms that need no more than admiration. Some are robust and flexible, happy to grow just about anywhere they're planted. Others are more temperamental, tending to sulk and droop if not pampered and petted.

The selection is more than enough to stump the beginning gardener or the flower enthusiast who hasn't much time to spend weeding, watering, and otherwise working in the garden. But that's what this bulletin is all about: narrowing down the selection. Easy-care perennials are terrific garden plants. They grow quickly, require little maintenance, and, for rent of a little space in your yard, remunerate you with bright blooms and gorgeous foliage year after year. No fuss, no muss, and plenty of beautiful flowers!

*A bed of perennials helps
a small specimen tree
blend into the landscape.*

Ten Easy-Care Perennials

Common Name	Genus
Astilbe	*Astilbe*
Blanketflower	*Gaillardia*
Black-eyed Susan	*Rudbeckia*
Coneflower	*Echinacea*
Coreopsis	*Coreopsis*
Daylily	*Hemerocallis*
Garden phlox	*Phlox*
Hosta	*Hosta*
Pincushion flower	*Scabiosa*
Stonecrop	*Sedum*

Why Perennials?

If you are new to the world of gardening or have grown only annuals in the past, you may not be aware of the many benefits that growing perennials can offer. Although perennials are often interplanted with annuals, they are certainly capable of standing alone. Indeed, many growers have gardens comprised entirely of perennials, and avid perennial fans wouldn't dream of growing anything but these wonderful plants.

Except in the more temperate zones, a perennial usually dies back each year after a hard frost and after freezing temperatures have set in. Some, like bleeding heart, go dormant in the summer. The following spring it sends up new green shoots and starts its growing and flowering cycle all over again. Some perennials live for only a few years, while others remain vital and attractive even when decades old.

Most perennials are self-propagating and multiply on their own, increasing in beauty and size each year. If they begin to overgrow their allotted space in the garden, they can usually be divided without too much trouble, then replanted elsewhere in the garden or shared with friends and fellow gardeners.

Though perennials initially cost more than annuals to purchase, they are actually less expensive over the long term, because you don't have to buy new ones every year, and if you want more plants, you can simply divide or take cuttings from your existing perennials. Growing perennials can also be a time saver, because they don't require replanting each year.

Many perennials — including the ones featured in this bulletin — are undemanding, wonderfully versatile, and adaptable to a variety of growing conditions. They can grow in poor soil or good soil and can survive both drought and overwatering, as long as they have drainage. Some perennials flourish in full sun, while others prefer deep shade, but generally all perennials can be grown in a partly shaded area. Though commonly thought of as garden bed plants, many species of perennials are suitable for growing in containers on a deck, porch, or patio. This versatility expands the growing options when gardening space is limited.

With their vivid colors, beautiful blooms, and bountiful foliage, perennials add exuberance and liveliness to the landscape.

Know Your Plants

It's important to know the definitions of the various plants. An *annual* completes its entire life cycle in one growing period: It grows, flowers, and dies all within one growing season. A *biennial* lives for two years, growing the first year, then blooming and dying the second. The wonderful *perennial* grows and blooms each and every year and forms seed with every blossom.

Ten Outstanding
Easy-Care Perennials

What makes these ten perennials the best in "easy care"? Not only are they beautiful and hardy, but they also have an undemanding nature, yielding great rewards for very little care. Most come in numerous varieties, offering a whole palette of colors and foliage for your garden design.

Astilbe (Astilbe spp.)

Prized for both its foliage and its flowers, astilbe is one of the most spectacular plants available for semishady places in the garden. Astilbes work well in the garden as border or accent plants, and when mass planted in groups of three or more, the effect is stunning. Astilbes also make excellent cut flowers, plus they dry attractively for dried flower arrangements. Some gardeners enjoy astilbe flowers during the winter by forcing a newly potted "start" taken from the mother plant after dormancy.

Astilbe has lovely, abundant, dark green fernlike foliage and produces flowers on long spikes, resembling feathery plumes, that soar over the leaves. Individual blossoms are minuscule, but each plume contains dozens of branches, with each branch bearing hundreds of flowers. Hardy in Zones 3 to 9, astilbe prefers partial shade, producing its most colorful flowers and lushest foliage when receiving morning sunshine and shade during the hottest part of the day. Astilbe prefers evenly moist soil that has been enriched with organic matter such as compost or leaf mold. Dry soil causes the plant to fade and wither. Depending on the

Growing at a Glance

HARDINESS:
Zones 3–9

SOIL REQUIREMENTS:
Moist, well-drained, humus-rich soil

LIGHT REQUIREMENTS:
Partial shade

WATER REQUIREMENTS:
Keep soil moist

SPACING REQUIREMENTS:
Set plants 18 to 24 inches (45–60 cm) apart

PROPAGATION:
By division in spring or fall

species and variety, the mound-shaped astilbe reaches from 1½ to 3 feet (45–90 cm) in height and spreads to 2 feet (60 cm) in width. Blooming time also depends on the variety, but each variety provides several weeks of color.

Astilbe is a heavy feeder and should be given a high-phosphorus fertilizer each spring. Because of rapid spreading, astilbe can quickly become overcrowded, resulting in sparse blooming. Rejuvenate the plants by dividing them in early spring or autumn every two to three years.

Astilbe is available in many varieties, including:

- *Astilbe* x *arendsii* 'Amethyst', an elegant lavender variety growing only 30 inches (75 cm) tall
- *Astilbe* x *arendsii* 'Fanal', which reaches over 2 feet (60 cm) in height and features scarlet blooms
- *Astilbe japonica* 'Deutschland', with brilliant white flowers
- *Astilbe* x *rosea* 'Peach Blossom', which blooms in — what else? — peach

Astilbe astilboides

Black-eyed Susan
(*Rudbeckia* spp.)

Black-eyed Susan has few rivals for its cheery, long-lasting color, even in the heat of the summer. Black-eyed Susans can be subjected to heat, drought, and neglect yet keep on blooming with vivid color.

The distinguishing characteristic of black-eyed Susan is its jaunty flower, which blooms from midsummer into autumn in Zones 4 to 9. The flowers are 3 inches or more in diameter, with petals of a bright, deep yellow color and a contrasting dome-shaped dark brown center. The foliage is clumping, with strong, slender stems reaching 2 to 2½ feet (60–75 cm) in height. The grayish green leaves have saw-toothed edges and are slightly hairy in appearance.

Black-eyed Susan is rarely bothered by pests or disease. If this perennial has a fault, it is that it spreads rapidly and needs to be divided every two to three years. Without root division, it can become over-crowded, resulting in a decrease in blooms. It may also become invasive.

Black-eyed Susans are wonderful for cutting; gather them up in large bouquets to bring color and cheer to your home. They are lovely when planted in drifts in beds and borders and are perfect for any place that needs a spot of added color. They prefer full sun but will tolerate partial shade, although if planted in shade they may not flower as profusely. They're not at all fussy about soil; the only requirement is that it be well drained. Space plants 12 to 18 inches (30–45 cm) apart, and water well after transplanting. Deadhead regularly to prolong blooming.

Growing at a Glance

HARDINESS:
Zones 4–9

SOIL REQUIREMENTS:
Fertile, well-drained soil

LIGHT REQUIREMENTS:
Full sun to partial shade

WATER REQUIREMENTS:
Low to moderate

SPACING REQUIREMENTS:
Set plants 12 to 18 inches (30–45 cm) apart

PROPAGATION:
By division in spring or fall, or by seed in spring

Some black-eyed Susan cultivars particularly favored by gardeners include:

- *R. fulgida* var. *sullivantii* 'Goldsturm', a popular choice commonly found at nurseries with large flowers on stems shorter than those of the species
- *R. laciniata* 'Goldquelle', bearing double flowers that smother the eye with yellow petals
- *R. laciniata* 'Golden Glow', another double black-eyed Susan with lots of yellow petals

Rudbeckia fulgida var. *sullivantii* 'Goldsturm'

Blanketflower (*Gaillardia* spp.)

Perfect when massed in borders, in cutting gardens, and as edging plants in shorter varieties, blanketflower is also suited for container growing. This species, which is actually a cross of two other species and a more vigorous performer than the natives, is very easily grown and floriferous, requiring only full sun and average, well-drained soil. Adequate drainage is essential, since blanketflower won't live with roots constantly wet roots.

Blanketflower's leaves are somewhat hairy and usually basal, forming a neat mound of foliage that is covered with blooms. The 3- to 4-inch (8–10 cm) daisylike flowers are displayed on graceful stems slightly above the foliage. They have dark, hairy centers and notched, banded petals. Deadheading promotes repeat blooming throughout the growing season. Each year the center of the plant crown dies back, and new plants appear slightly off center the following spring. The new plants are easily transplanted and usually bloom the same year. Hardy in Zones 3 to 8, blanketflowers are very attractive to bees and butterflies.

A number of perennial varieties are available, with new types showing up each year. Two *G. grandiflora* strains are particularly popular: 'Goblin', a dwarf variety some 12 inches (30 cm) high and wide, has vivid red flowers with yellow tips; Monarch Hybrids feature blooms in various shades of red, yellow, and brown. 'Burgundy' has deep wine-red blooms, reaches 20 to 24 inches (50–60 cm) in height, and spreads 16 to 20 inches (40–50 cm).

Gaillardia spp.

☼Growing at a Glance

HARDINESS:
Zones 3–8

SOIL REQUIREMENTS:
Well-drained soil

LIGHT REQUIREMENTS:
Full sun

WATER REQUIREMENTS:
Low

SPACING REQUIREMENTS:
Set plants 18 to 24 inches (45–60 cm) apart

PROPAGATION:
By seed or division in spring, or by root cuttings in winter

Coneflower
(Echinacea purpurea)

A lovely American native of the prairies, coneflower — also known as echinacea — has become popular for its potent immune-building properties. Echinacea is an incredibly tough, long-lived, and easy-to-grow perennial. Wonderful in a wildflower garden or natural landscape, coneflowers also perform beautifully in the back of a flower bed. They act as magnets to butterflies and entice them to visit the garden, adding another element of enjoyment. And as cut flowers they are long lasting and easy to arrange because of their long stems. If these wonderful plants have a fault, it's that they may require staking.

Hardy in Zones 3 to 8 and drought resistant, they grow in nearly any garden soil that is well drained. While they prefer full sun, coneflowers thrive in partial shade as well.

Coneflowers reach 3 to 4 feet (90–120 cm) high and spread to 18 inches (45 cm) wide, growing in a clump. The foliage is hairy and roughly toothed, with alternate leaves. The daisylike flowers often reach 4 inches (10 cm) in diameter — 6 inches (15 cm) is possible — and are displayed on long stems rising well above the foliage. Each stem exhibits a single blossom with colorful petals that curve backward to display the cone-shaped center: stiff, pin-shaped, orange-colored disk flowers rising from a brownish center that becomes increasingly conical as the bloom matures. Interesting to observe and touch, these cones work nicely in dried flower arrangements.

Though commonly thought of as blooming only in purple, coneflowers come in a variety of cultivars. 'White Lustre', 'White

Growing at a Glance

HARDINESS: Zones 3–8	**WATER REQUIREMENTS:** Heavy
SOIL REQUIREMENTS: Well-drained, humus-rich soil	**SPACING REQUIREMENTS:** Set plants 18 to 24 inches (45–60 cm) apart
LIGHT REQUIREMENTS: Prefers full sun but tolerates partial shade	**PROPAGATION:** By seed in spring, or by division in spring or fall

Swan', and 'Alba' are white varieties; 'Bright Star' bears maroon flowers; and 'Magnus' is a profuse bloomer in a carmine rose color.

Coneflowers are best propagated in early spring or autumn by division. New plants can also be started from seed. Set plants 18 inches apart in the garden, or grow them in a container that has adequate drainage. Although removing the spent flower heads produces more flowering, leaving some to dry in place provides late-season interest in the garden and gives visiting birds something to feast on.

Echinacea purpurea

Coreopsis
(Coreopsis spp.)

If you want a plant that can take adverse growing conditions and still bloom merrily all summer long, the cheerful coreopsis is the answer. Coreopsis produces abundant daisylike flowers on wiry stems that rise above the foliage. Although the blooms are commonly seen in shades of yellow, gold, and orange, lovely pink varieties are also available. Coreopsis quickly fills containers or baskets, brightening porches or patios. It can also be cut and brought inside for fresh flower arrangements. Coreopsis is perfect in a border or as an edging plant.

Growing at a Glance

HARDINESS:
Zones 4–9

SOIL REQUIREMENTS:
Fertile, well-drained soil

LIGHT REQUIREMENTS:
Full sun to partial shade

WATER REQUIREMENTS:
Heavy

SPACING REQUIREMENTS:
Set plants 12 to 18 inches (30–45 cm) apart

PROPAGATION:
By seed or division in spring

Not fussy about soil, mildew resistant, and hardy in Zones 4 to 9,
this plant requires full sun and
can withstand heat, drought,
and — here's the best part —
neglect. Removing the spent
flowers prolongs blooming
throughout most of the
growing season. The fo-
liage, which forms a neat,
rapidly spreading clump,
can have oval-shaped or
fernlike leaves, depending on
the variety. Space plants 12 to 18
inches apart for a solid mass of color. In
a reasonably good soil, fertilization is not
required.

If you wish to propagate coreopsis, it's
easy to do in the spring by division, but division is rarely needed. Plants can also be
started from seed.

*Coreopsis
tinctoria*

There are many varieties of coreopsis to
choose from. Some of the more popular varieties include:

- *C. auriculata* 'Nana', which reaches 8 inches (20 cm) in
  height and bears yellow-orange flowers
- *C. grandiflora* 'Sunray', which has double golden yellow
  flowers
- *C. lanceolata* 'Brown Eyes', bearing golden flowers with a
  ring of maroon in the center
- *C. rosea*, which bears small pink flowers on 24-inch (60 cm)
  stems
- *C. rosea* 'American Dream', featuring pink flowers with
  yellow centers
- *C. tinctoria*, which usually features bright yellow flower-
  heads with dark red centers but also comes in dark red,
  purple, and brown varieties
- *C. verticillata* 'Moonbeam', which has lemon yellow flowers
  and fernlike foliage on 18-inch (45 cm) stems

Daylily
(*Hemerocallis* spp.)

The common tawny daylily and lemon daylily were two of the first flowers brought to American colonial gardens several hundred years ago. Today there are thousands of varieties to pick from, with more being introduced each year. Sometimes entire gardens are planted using only these marvelous plants. Daylilies are also wonderful for naturalizing.

Though each colorful flower lasts only one day — hence the name — they are borne in a profuse succession of blooms for several weeks on tall stalks that rise from the clumps of foliage. Daylilies bloom from late spring to autumn. Some cultivars will repeat bloom a second time during a single season. Very easy to grow, daylilies require only good, well-drained soil and lots of sun. In very hot areas, they benefit from light shading in the afternoon. They are available in numerous sizes and are hardy in Zones 3 to 10.

Flowers range from 3 to 8 inches, and many are fragrant. A vast variety of flower colors is available, some with freckled petals and contrasting colors in the center and on the tips of the stamens. Some cultivars have double flowers. The thick, sword-shaped, basal foliage is attractive even when the plant is not in bloom.

Hemerocallis spp.

Daylilies grow from tuberous, fleshy roots, and many multiply quickly. Propagation in spring or autumn by division is most common, although new plants can be attained by sowing from seed. When buying a clump, look for plants that have at least two "fans," or sets of leaves. This means that the plant is large enough to bloom the first season after planting. Plant at least 18 inches (45 cm) apart to permit spreading and lush growth. Divide when the clump appears overcrowded or blooms are sparse.

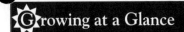

Growing at a Glance

HARDINESS:
Zones 3–10

SOIL REQUIREMENTS:
Fertile, moist, well-drained soil

LIGHT REQUIREMENTS:
Full sun to light shade

WATER REQUIREMENTS:
Heavy

SPACING REQUIREMENTS:
Set plants 18 inches (45 cm) apart

PROPAGATION:
By seed or division in spring or fall

With their shrubby foliage and beautiful blooms, daylilies make wonderful borders for pathways.

Some noteworthy daylilies are:

- 'Stella de Oro', 2 feet (60 cm) tall with golden yellow flowers
- 'Perfect Peach Glory', a beautiful peachy pink and, like 'Stella de Oro', a long-season bloomer
- 'Catherine Woodbury' and 'Princeton Silky', both tall and elegant with pink blooms
- 'Fine Frenzy', a lovely combination of mauve petals with a gold throat and white midribs
- 'Happy Returns', a miniature long bloomer

If red daylilies are your passion, try:

- 'Autumn Red' or 'Chicago Fire', both tall varieties
- 'Ed Murray', a very deep black-red
- 'Breakout', wine red with ruffled petals
- 'Little Missy', a miniature red
- *H. fulva* is the old-fashioned tawny daylily, perfect for naturalizing or for erosion control on steep slopes

Garden Phlox
(Phlox paniculata)

Unlike its cousin creeping phlox *(P. stolonifera)*, garden phlox is a tall, elegant plant that is perfect in gardens where height is needed. Heavily floriferous and fragrant, this plant is wonderful as an accent, for defining a border, or in the rear of a bed. Garden phlox makes marvelous cut flowers, as well. It is easy to grow in rich, well-drained soil in full sun to partial shade — propagate from seed or by root division — and benefits from watering during hot weather. Garden phlox sometimes requires staking or support, and though it is prone to mildew in humid areas, this can be reduced by keeping individual plants at least 2 feet (60 cm) apart to encourage air circulation. Deadhead spent flowers to promote blooming.

Garden phlox has lance-shaped leaves and very strong stems that form clumps, but its real beauty lies in its flowers, which are breathtaking. Three-quarter-inch flowers are massed in showy pyramid-shaped clusters 12 to 18 inches (30–45 cm) long, rising above the foliage in an array of brilliant color. Dividing plants every three to four years in the spring or fall keeps them vigorous and blooming lavishly.

HARDINESS:	WATER REQUIREMENTS:
Zones 4–8	Heavy
SOIL REQUIREMENTS:	SPACING REQUIREMENTS:
Fertile, well-drained soil	Set plants 2 to 3 feet (60–90 cm) apart
LIGHT REQUIREMENTS:	
Full sun to partial shade	PROPAGATION:
	By division in spring or fall

Hardy in zones 4 to 8, garden phlox is available in an amazing range of colors, from the delicate to the bold — from white through pinks and reds and lavenders and purples, often with a contrasting "eye," or center. Some notable cultivars are:

- 'Robert Poore', reaching 5 feet (1.5 m) high and 3 feet (.9 m) wide, with hot-pink flowers that fill the top 18 to 20 inches (45–50 cm) of each stem.
- 'Laura', which is purple with a cream-colored center and reaches 3½ to 4 feet (1–1.2 m) tall
- 'Katherine', violet with a white center, growing 3½ to 4 feet (1–1.2 m) high
- 'David', brilliant pure white and exceptionally fragrant, growing up to 4 feet (1.2 m) tall
- 'Tenor', which has bright scarlet flowers with a spicy aroma and grows up to 4 feet (1.2 m) high
- 'Caroline Vandenburg' is a soft blue color, reaching 40 to 48 inches (1–1.2 m) in height
- 'Bright Eyes', with deep pink blossoms and red centers

Phlox paniculata

Hosta (*Hosta* spp.)

For lush foliage, few garden plants can compete with the carefree hosta. These hardy perennials form attractive mounds of foliage ranging from 18 inches (45 cm) all the way up to 6 feet (180 cm) in diameter, depending on the species and cultivar. Extremely durable, these plants can thrive for 20 years with no special care, except perhaps occasional dividing. Because of their adaptability and versatility, hostas are often used as ground covers, in the foreground or background of a bed, as edging plants, or as a simple but striking specimen plant. Smaller varieties are content growing in containers.

Most hostas have deeply veined, pointed or heart-shaped basal leaves. Some of the newer cultivars' leaves are lance shaped. Hosta leaves may be smooth or crinkled with defined or wavy edges. The foliage comes in a variety of colors: golden yellow to pale green to deep jade, many shades of blue, and variegated patterns of yellow or green and white. The variegated varieties and the blues are most colorful when grown in partially shaded areas that receive morning or late-afternoon sun. Though not grown specifically for their flowers, hostas produce clusters of lavender or white flower spikes in the summer.

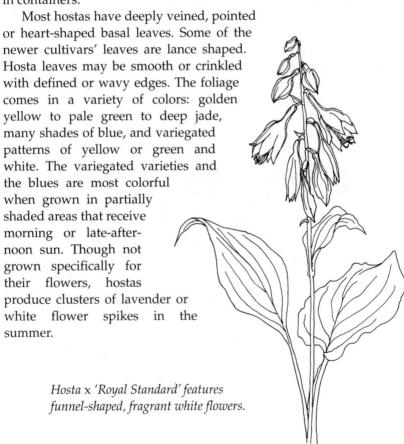

Hosta x *'Royal Standard' features funnel-shaped, fragrant white flowers.*

HARDINESS:
Zones 3–8

SOIL REQUIREMENTS:
Fertile, well-drained soil

LIGHT REQUIREMENTS:
Partial to full shade

WATER REQUIREMENTS:
Heavy

SPACING REQUIREMENTS:
Set plants 1 to 4 feet (30–120 cm) apart, depending on the species

PROPAGATION:
By division in spring or late summer

There are over 1,000 varieties of this wonderful plant to choose from. Miniature varieties grow less than 12 inches (30 cm) in height and width, medium varieties average 14 inches (35 cm) high and 18 inches (45 cm) wide, medium-large varieties grow 18 inches (45 cm) high and spread 2 to 3 feet (60–90 cm), and large varieties grow over 2 feet (60 cm) tall and often spread to 6 feet (1.8 m) in diameter.

Hostas perform best in moist but well-drained garden soil enriched with plenty of compost or leaf mold. They prefer partial

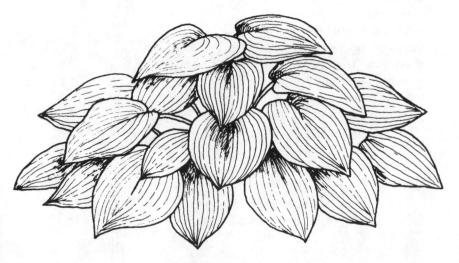

Hosta x *'August Moon'*

shade, and though they can thrive in full shade, their growth may not be as lush. In cooler areas of the country, they can survive in full sun, but the foliage may sunburn or bleach if exposed directly to hot sun. In warmer climates, approximately one to two hours of summer sun is the limit. Hostas are hardy in Zones 3 to 8 and need a period of dormancy with freezing temperatures in the winter.

Established hosta plants can be propagated in early spring or late summer by dividing the clumps. Keep the new starts well watered until they are established. Slugs are hostas' greatest nemesis — aside from deer, which apparently consider hosta leaves and flowers a delicacy — and the plants seem to attract them. To deter slugs, circle the plant with copper tape or foil, available at garden centers.

Pincushion Flower (Scabiosa caucasica)

Commonly called pincushion flower because of the flower head's appearance when closed, the profuse, lacy blooms of Caucasian scabious have delighted gardeners since it was introduced to England in 1803. With regular deadheading, the plant blooms with waves of color practically nonstop from late spring to autumn.

Extremely easy to grow and floriferous, pincushion flower requires only good, well-drained soil in a sunny place — though afternoon shade in hotter climates encourages longer blooming.

Pincushion flower forms a neat and attractive clump with lance-shaped, deeply cut leaves and long, graceful stems. Because of its habits and form, *S. caucasica* is particularly versatile — wonderful for use as edging plants, in border gardens, to define a walkway or path, or for growing in containers. The long stems also make them excellent cut flowers, and they are especially beautiful when planted in drifts. The

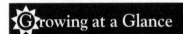

Growing at a Glance

HARDINESS:
Zones 3–7

SOIL REQUIREMENTS:
Well-drained, neutral to slightly alkaline soil

LIGHT REQUIREMENTS:
Full sun

WATER REQUIREMENTS:
Heavy

SPACING REQUIREMENTS:
Depends on the species

PROPAGATION:
By seed or division in spring

dome-shaped blossoms are thickly fringed with petals, and the lighter-colored, textured centers are of visual interest. The blossoms average 3 inches (8 cm) in diameter and are available in several cool pastel colors. Butterflies love pincushion flower and are drawn to it, enhancing the garden even further.

Pincushion flower can be propagated by division or started from seed in the spring. The plant is hardy in Zones 3 to 7 and is rarely bothered by pests or disease.

Some notable *S. caucasica* varieties, which reach 1½ to 2 feet (45–60 cm) in height and 14 to 18 inches (35–45 cm) in width, include:

- 'Alba' and 'Miss Willmott', both blooming white
- 'Fama', very attractive, long-lasting flowers colored true lavender
- 'Butterfly Blue', very easy to grow with lavender-blue flowers

Scabiosa caucasica

Showy Stonecrop
(Sedum spectabile)

For late-season blooming from late summer through fall and interesting displays in the winter months, consider this marvelous plant. One of the easiest of all perennials to grow, it is drought resistant and rarely bothered by pests or disease if grown in slightly dry soil. Showy stonecrop is excellent in the garden bed or in borders — it's exceptional when planted in masses. After the flowers have turned brown, they can be cut and used inside in dried arrangements.

Showy stonecrop has creamy bluish green foliage that forms large, neat clumps. The opposite or whorled leaves and stems are smooth and succulent, inviting touch. Flat heads of flower buds appear in midsummer and start out bluish green like the foliage. As the growing season progresses, the flowers open and turn first salmon pink, then a rich mahogany color. Left alone, they turn brown and remain attractive throughout the winter.

This lovely perennial is hardy in Zones 4 to 9, and although it prefers full sun, it also grows in partial shade. It's not at all fussy about soil or fertilization, and any average soil with good drainage will make it happy. Plant propagation is easy by stem cuttings.

Some notable varieties of *Sedum spectabile* are:

- 'Brilliant', an early bloomer with bright pink flowers
- 'Meteor', which grows only to 18 inches and features vivid pink flowers
- 'StarDust', with white to very pale pink blossoms and pale green leaves
- 'Variegatum', a neat-growing plant with pink blossoms and leaves touched with creamy white

Sedum spectabile

Choosing the Right Location for Perennials

Although perennials are very adaptable, they need to be planted in a spot that meets their growing preferences to ensure lush growth and flowering.

Perennials that prefer full sun need to receive at least eight hours of sunshine a day. Perennials that prefer partial shade can be grown in an area that receives five to six hours of sunshine and dappled shade the rest of the day. In hot climates, the amount of shade received should be increased to 7 to 8 hours. Most shade-loving perennials will also grow in dappled shade, but they should be located where they are shaded during the hottest part of the day.

Perennials are easiest to care for when they are planted in conditions that suit them. Perennials that prefer shade, for example, will do best beneath trees, shrubs, or a sheltering wall or arbor.

Of course you'll want to plant your perennials in an area that is clearly visible, so they can be admired. However, you also want to be sure that the perennial bed is located in an area that is convenient to tend. This makes chores like watering and weeding easier.

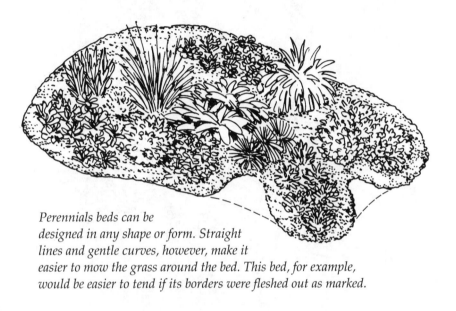

Perennials beds can be designed in any shape or form. Straight lines and gentle curves, however, make it easier to mow the grass around the bed. This bed, for example, would be easier to tend if its borders were fleshed out as marked.

Preparing a New Perennial Bed

Even though most perennials are tough and hardy, properly prepared soil promotes healthy growth, longevity, and the most attractive foliage and blooms. Taking the time to properly prepare the soil before planting will save you work later, get your perennials off to a good start, and help them have a long, productive life.

To prepare a planting bed, first remove any sod from the area; then dig the soil to a depth of at least 12 inches (30 cm). Remove any rocks, and break up large clumps of soil. Test the soil for pH and nutrient levels. Add fertilizers or soil conditioners if needed.

To prepare a planting bed, first demarcate its borders. Then dig out the soil within the planned bed to a depth of 12 inches.

Using Fertilizers and Soil Conditioners

Fertilizers (both organic and inorganic) supply nutrients to plants. The three major nutrients are nitrogen, phosphorus, and potassium, usually identified on fertilizer containers by the symbols N, P, and K, respectively. Most perennials thrive in soil that has equal levels of NPK. Soil pH can also affect plant growth. Most perennials prefer a soil that is near neutral or slightly acidic. A soil with a pH of 6.0 to 7.0 doesn't require any adjustment for growing most perennials. The best way to determine precisely what your soil needs is through soil testing. Test kits are available from many garden-supply shops, or you can send a sample to a laboratory for analysis, often through your county cooperative extension service. Many universities also offer soil testing for a nominal fee.

Soil conditioners improve the soil's texture or consistency. Soil that's mostly heavy clay is not desirable for growing, nor is soil that's mostly sand. Ideal soil is rich and loamy, made up of 50 percent organic and mineral matter (a blend of silt, sand, or clay), 25 percent air space, and 25 percent water. Some commonly used soil conditioners that add organic matter are leaf mold, compost, peat moss, and rotted cow manure. Fortunately, these soil conditioners also add nutrients. Builder's sand, perlite, or vermiculite in combination with organic matter is used to lighten heavy clay soils and improve aeration.

Adding fertilizer and a conditioner like leaf mold to the soil will encourage healthy, hardy perennials.

After adding soil conditioners and fertilizers, dig or rototill the bed again to thoroughly mix the additives into the soil. Let the soil rest for a couple of days, watering lightly each day. This gives the soil time to adjust before planting. It also gives any uprooted weed seeds a chance to sprout so that they can be removed.

Buying High-Quality Plants

Perennials can be purchased from local nurseries and growers, by mail order from catalogs, or via the Internet. When you're purchasing mail order plants, you won't be able to examine individual specimens and will have to rely on the supplier for high-quality plants. When buying perennials from a nursery, however, you have more say in what you will and won't bring home.

If you want blooms the first year, choose perennials that are at least one year old. Select plants that are compact and stocky with strong stems. And since healthy, vital plants that were given good care stand a better chance of growing and thriving when planted in your garden, avoid plants that exhibit the following signs:

- **Parched soil and wilted or sun-scorched leaves** are a sign of neglect. Each time a plant becomes badly wilted or stressed, it loses vitality and becomes more susceptible to disease or insect infestations.
- **Roots growing through the bottom of the container** indicates that the plant is probably root bound and has been in the container too long.
- **Tall, spindly plants with sparse foliage** indicate that the plant has been grown in low light or crowded conditions and is probably weak.
- **Holes in the leaves, chewed foliage, stickiness, and scales or webs on the leaves or stems** are all signs of insect infestation. Do not bring these plants home under any circumstances, even if they're free.

Transplanting to the Garden

If possible, transplant your perennials to the garden on an overcast or partly cloudy day. If the forecast is full sun for weeks, plant in the early evening.

Nursery Plants

Dig a planting hole that is somewhat larger in diameter than the nursery pot. Make the hole just deep enough that the perennial will be at the same depth at which it is growing in the pot. Water the soil in the pot thoroughly, then gently pull the plant from the pot, holding the plant at its base, where plant meets soil. Set the plant in the hold, gently firm the soil around the roots, and water well.

For the first two or three days after transplanting, use newspaper or an overturned bushel basket to protect the tender transplants from sun and wind.

Mail-Order Plants

Mail-order plants are often shipped bare root, that is, without soil. If the plants remain dormant, being shipped bare root won't harm them. However, if the temperature in a truck or cargo bay is warm, the plants may break dormancy and begin to grow. Without soil and water, they won't last very long. If the plants are not in good condition when you receive them, return them to the mail-order supplier.

Bare-root plants should be packed in organic mulch and wrapped in plastic. Check the roots for damage; if the roots are broken or show signs of mold or decay, return the plants to the supplier.

Thankfully, most mail-order plants arrive at your doorstep while still dormant. Ideally, bare-root plants should be planted immediately. If you're not able to plant them for a few days, do not disturb their protective packaging material other than to trickle over their roots a tiny amount of water — just enough to moisten the roots. Place the plants back in the shipping container and store the container in a cool, dry, dark location.

Bare-root plants can be treated just like nursery plants for transplanting. Look for the soil line on the plant's stem to determine proper planting depth.

Maintenance through the Seasons

Keep perennials thoroughly watered during their first season in the garden. After the first year, they can take care of themselves, except during drought conditions. Watering deeply during this first year encourages root growth and helps establish the plant. Ideally, soak the soil to a depth of 6 to 8 inches (15–20 cm); shallow watering encourages shallow root development. Mulch around the plants to help them retain soil moisture and to discourage weed growth.

Fertilizing

Feeding perennials lightly two or three times during the growing season encourages growth and flowering. A general balanced fertilizer like 5-10-10 works well. If you use organic fertilizers, apply appropriately to provide similar nutrition.

Deadheading

Removing faded and spent blossoms can encourage rebloom and stronger vegetative growth. Don't deadhead if you wish to save the seeds, however, since deadheading prevents the plant from producing seeds. Many birds relish the seeds of perennial flowers, so sparing spent blossoms will make your avian visitors happy.

Cutting Back

Though it's not absolutely necessary, cutting perennials nearly to the ground in late autumn has advantages. Cutting back can:

- Improve the appearance of the flower bed or plant by removing the dead foliage.
- Make weeds easier to see and remove. Dig them out now so they won't compete with the plant's new growth in the springtime.

- Make mulching easier. If you live in an area that has alternate periods of freezing and thawing or severe cold, winter mulch can help protect the roots and prevent heaving from the soil temperature fluctuations. Apply mulch after the soil has had at least one hard frost.

Always leave a few inches of foliage or stems when cutting back to avoid injuring the crowns. These stems also help identify the plants' locations should you wish to dig in the bed before the perennials begin growing again.

Plant Propagation

Collecting, storing, and sowing seed is a time-honored method of plant propagation. However, seeds do not always produce uniform crops, nor do they always "take" readily. Happily, many perennials can be easily cloned, or propagated, by division or by stem cuttings.

Dividing

Some plants possess specialized stems and roots whose functions are food storage and natural vegetative reproduction. These stems or roots can be separated by various methods summarily called *division*. Perennials that spread abundantly need to be dug up and divided every few years. This will not only keep the plants from becoming invasive but also help rejuvenate them. The additional plants, or "starts," obtained from division can be replanted elsewhere or shared with gardening friends.

Common Perennials That Can Be Divided

Aster	Evening primrose
Astilbe	False indigo
Beardtongue	Gayfeather
Bellflower	Hosta
Black-eyed Susan	Lavender
Blanket flower	Pasque flower
Bleeding-heart	Peony
Catmint	Phlox
Coneflower	Pincushion flower
Coreopsis	Yarrow
Daylily	

Crown Division of Perennials

The *crown* is that area of the plant near the surface of the ground from which new shoots grow. Many of these shoots also have roots. To propagate them, just separate and transplant the plants.

A general rule of thumb for crown division of perennials is that summer- and autumn-flowering perennials should be divided in early spring or late autumn, while spring-flowering perennials should be divided only in autumn. Summer and winter dividing should be avoided because of the undue stress it places on plants.

1. Water and loosen the soil around both the plant and the new planting bed before you dig out the plant.

2. With a garden fork, lever the plant out of the soil.

3. Pull apart small crowns with your hands. For large crowns, use the tines of a hand fork to gently pry apart clumps of three or four stem clumps from the main crown.

4. Transplant each new start into a hole that is larger than the sprawling roots. Spread the roots evenly over the bottom of the hole.

5. Fill the hole with loose soil. Water well and mulch.

Dividing Perennials with Rhizomes

Many perennials, including daylilies and many irises, produce rhizomes. Rhizomes are large, fleshy stems that grow underground and store food for the plant. Both the plant's aboveground foliage and flowers and its belowground root system stem from the rhizome. Rhizome division should be undertaken in late summer or early fall.

1. Dig up the entire clump, and shake gently to remove as much dirt as possible to enable you to better see the rhizome.

2. Using a sharp knife, cut the rhizome so that each piece has at least one bud. Trim back any foliage to 3 inches to encourage rooting before replanting.

3. Let the rhizomes air dry for an hour or so to seal the cut area.

4. Replant in fertile ground with the rhizome covered by half an inch to an inch of soil.

Taking Stem Cuttings

Stem cuttings are the type of cutting most folks first experiment with, because many herbaceous plants, such as the zonal geranium, root so easily that a glass of water is an acceptable propagation medium. To take a stem cutting, follow these simple steps.

Common Perennials That Can Be Propagated by Stem Cuttings

Balloon flower	Jacob's ladder
Delphinium	Sage
Geranium	Showy stonecrop

---

1. Mix equal parts of perlite, vermiculite, and peat moss in a small, sterilized container. Water well. Using your finger or pencil, poke a hole in the middle of this rooting medium.

2. Select a plant that is actively growing with young and succulent stems. Choose a stem that has several leaf nodes, side shoots, or growing buds 3 to 6 inches (8–15 cm) long, and cut from the parent plant with a sharp knife, close to the main stalk.

3. Bring the cutting inside the house immediately, and recut with the cleanest slice possible, just below the bottom node. A razor blade works well because it avoids either crushing the stem or leaving strands of plant tissue hanging.

4. Remove leaves from the lower half of the stem.

5. Dip the base of the cutting into a rooting powder. (Rooting powder is most often a blend of an inert powder, plant hormones to hasten root formation in the cuttings, and a fungicide to help prevent disease while the cuttings are rooting.). Insert the cutting into the medium, one quarter its length, and gently firm the medium around it.

6. Water thoroughly and then cover with a plastic bag to form a mini-greenhouse over the cutting. Use sticks, twigs, or wires around the container edge to keep the plastic from touching the cutting. Disposable chopsticks work well; they're sturdy and easily poke into the growing medium. Place the cutting in a location with good light but not direct sun, at about 70° to 80°F.

Strip the lower leaves from the stem before planting.

7. Encourage air circulation by lifting the plastic for about an hour each day. Water as needed with lukewarm water. Be careful not to overwater.

8. Rooting usually takes place in 6 to 8 weeks. After this time, lift the cutting out gently to check for roots. When roots are approximately 1 inch (3 cm) long, transplant the cutting into a small pot with good growing soil.

A sunny windowsill is an ideal location for a stem-cutting plastic greenhouse.